CW00482692

LOVE FOR GOD AND
LOVE FOR ONE ANOTHER

Mohammad Ali Shomali

Wings of Unity Series, Part Two:

LOVE FOR GOD AND
LOVE FOR ONE ANOTHER

Mohammad Ali Shomali

ISBN: 978-1-904934-29-5

© Institute of Islamic Studies, 2017

First published in Great Britain in 2017

Institute of Islamic Studies

140 Maida Vale, London W9 1QB

Tel: (44) 0207 604 5500; Fax: (44) 0207 604 4898

Email: icel@ic-el.com

Contents

In the Name of God, the Compassionate, the Merciful

Foreword

It is with great pleasure that I present this small book to our dear readers. This work contains the text of my presentation, as well as the discussions that took place afterwards, from the second round of Wings of Unity, held on January 14, 2017. The second part of the book is a brief report on the events around Wings of Unity II which was published in the March 2017 issue of *Islam Today*. On January 12, 2017, a Q&A session was held at Sophia Institute University for staff, students and inhabitants of Loppiano. The event was named, "Frontiers of Interreligious Dialogue." Thanks to God, this session went very well. A summary of the Q&A can be found in this report.

The ideas presented in this work can be better understood after reading the first volume of Wings of Unity: *Unity of God and Unity in God*. It should also be noted that Wings of Unity sessions are meant to be an opportunity for a group of Christians and Muslims who have known each other for many years, built a strong sense of trust overtime, and are also deeply committed to the ideal of unity in their theology and spirituality to share their ideas and, more importantly, to *think together*. It is a kind of laboratory where we are not hesitant to raise our concerns and discuss our ideas even if they are not well-developed and finalized. Therefore, readers are expected to bear in mind the context of these discussions and not to attribute ideas mentioned in this book to those who are mentioned by name in this volume without consulting them and taking their consent, especially since this is the draft edition and is mostly for internal use.

I take this opportunity to thank God for all His blessings and in particular for our friendship and fraternal love. I thank all of the Christian and Muslim participants of Wings of Unity I and II. My special thanks go to Professor Piero Coda for welcoming the idea of Wings of Unity in the first place and for the openness and warmth of his spirit. I should thank Sister Israa Safieddine who transcribed and edited the lectures. I also thank Sister Hanieh Tarkian for translating and transcribing the comments following my presentation which were made in Italian. I take this opportunity to thank both of them and pray to God for their success.

Mohammad Ali Shomali

17th August 2017

Love for God and

Love for One Another[1]

Introduction

I am very grateful to be given this blessing of meeting once again here at Sophia University Institute. Although we are involved in many interfaith activities throughout the year, this project is at the top of my list of priorities in interfaith activities. I hope and pray that we will be able to hold these meetings again and again. I pray that God will point us in the best direction.

After a very rich discussion with Piero in the morning, it's very difficult for me to talk. I hope that what I say will be of benefit to you. I ask God for help.

Before starting, however, I'd like to share some news. I think that in addition to our discussions in Wings of Unity, it's also a good opportunity to share news of what will take place in between these meetings.

Thanks to God, we had a very good meeting with some of the Shi'a members of our community in Glasgow in

[1] This lecture was delivered on January 14, 2017 at Sophia University Institute in Loppiano, Italy as part of the second round of Wings of Unity.

7

September. A conference on peace and unity was held at the City Hall, with over 200 people from Shiʻa, Sunni, Christian, and other communities. Officials from political parties, the police, and the army were also in attendance. Our Focolare friends from Glasgow were also present. After several presentations, my role was to appear in a panel for question-and-answer. I shared a few general ideas on interfaith dialogue, as well as some thoughts on interfaith and the environment. The ideas were well-received.

Later, in November, the Shiʻa and the Focolare of Glasgow met with each other. It was a very good day for me; I wanted them to work together. They met at the Focolare House in Glasgow and it was there that they decided to invite me once again to Glasgow. They were brainstorming ideas for programs and one of the things they came up with was to arrange a "Time for Reflection" with the Scottish Parliament. One of the Focolare members who has ties with someone in the Parliament had proposed my name, and they have since officially invited me to speak at the Scottish Parliament in February. I hope to take this message of unity to the Scottish Parliament.[2][3]

---

[2] This talk was delivered on February 28, 2017 and is available here: https://youtu.be/1F5WvJ3ohVU. The text of the speech can be found here: https://www.theyworkforyou.com/sp/?id=2017-02-28.0.2

[3] In addition to the speech at the Scottish Parliament in Edinburgh, the Ahl Al Bait Society of Scotland and the Focolare Movement in Scotland jointly organized an open lecture on interfaith at the University of Glasgow centered around the following theme: *Unity in God and Unity of God*. The speakers were Dr. Shomali and Dr. Paolo Frizzi, a lecturer in

A few days ago I was also contacted by the secretariat for Iran's Book of the Year Award, which is a prestigious event in which the best writers are awarded by our president. It has been going on for many years. This year they are introducing a special award for interfaith activities, and they chose me and Abbot Timothy Wright[4] as the award winners for the first award that they will present. God-willing, on February 6, 2017, we will go together and receive this award from the president of Iran, which I think is a good way to promote interreligious activities. I think it will be inspiring for people to witness a Catholic monk dressed in his habit receiving an award from a Shi'a cleric who is president.[5]

Lastly, in March we will be holding a training course in Switzerland for members of our community. We will be the same team – Mahnaz, Shahnaze, Israa, and I – along with 18 people from the UK and North America. We will spend four days in Geneva with the World Council of Churches and

---

Interreligious Dialogue, and Religions and Global Processes in Italy at the Sophia University Institute. To see a report on this trip, please refer to:
http://www.focolare.org/gb/news/2017/03/16/scotland-giving-unity-wings/

[4] Abbot Timothy Wright is a Catholic monk from England who invited Dr. Shomali on multiple occasions to visit Ampleforth Abbey many years ago.

[5] To read more about the award, please refer to:
http://islam-today.co.uk/special-award-for-interreligious-dialogue-islam-and-christianity

then go to Montet.[6] I thought that this would be the best way to run a course on interfaith; for participants to not only learn and discuss theories, but to also see the realities of the church for themselves and have the opportunity to ask Christians directly. I'm also excited to go to Montet. I've never been there before. I'll be sure to take Loppiano's greetings to Montet.[7]

Love for God leading to love for others

Now, what I thought would be good to discuss today is how loving God should lead to loving others. Although many people have in one way or another experienced love in God, it is unfortunate that in this day and age atheism is on the rise. Perhaps never in the history of humanity has there been such a high percentage of atheists in the world. Many people are also reportedly interested in spirituality but a spirituality that is devoid of God or religion. This is very sad.

Those who don't love God suffer

I think that people who don't have God in their lives do not know what gift they are missing out on. We also don't know how much they suffer. When someone lacks God in his or her life, it is far more difficult than being an orphan in the

---

[6] Montet is a small Swiss village which houses one of the many Focolare towns worldwide. The center in Montet offers formation courses for members of the Focolare Movement.

[7] A report on this visit, published in the May 2017 issue of *Islam Today*, can be found here:
http://islam-today.co.uk/interfaith-engagement-in-theory-practice-switzerland-2017

sense of having no mother, no father, no grandmother, and no grandfather; lacking God is more painful than being orphaned from every direction.

I believe that part of the problem – not all of the problem – is that as religious people, we have failed to properly demonstrate the beauty of faith to others.

On the one hand, the sad reality is that we've been so preoccupied with our differences that we neglected to work together and offer our testimony to others. This is while we know that clashes between religious people are used as an excuse by some people to say goodbye to religion and to God.

Two types of love for God

On the other hand, there is the sad reality of what happens among many religious people, which is to imagine that they have love for God. They may claim to love God, but it's not a true love for God. True love comes with humility and a dissolving of the ego. Unfortunately what we see is that some people use their supposed love for God as an excuse to develop a bigger ego in themselves; they believe themselves to be superior to others, and they unjustly and unjustifiably claim that they have a monopoly over God. This is especially dangerous because while people can give themselves the right to do all sorts of bad things, when someone puts himself in the position of speaking on behalf of God there is no limit to the amount of harm they can cause. As a human being, there is a limit to my influence on others; I may claim that I'm superior because of my race, ethnicity, intelligence, and so forth, and through it make a case for ruling others. But if I claim to be a spokesperson for God – in other words, I have an exclusive connection to God – then I can easily give myself the right to make all kinds of decisions. I can even make decisions about whether others can have a place of worship and whether to destroy or save lives. I can be very, very dangerous.

When you look at these people, they seem to be very religious, but only on the surface. For example, from a Muslim's perspective, you might see that they have a beard, they wear a certain outfit, they always go to religious gatherings, they pray, they fast, and so on. On the surface, everything looks religious, but you don't sense that vibe and fragrance that comes from a person who is connected to God. You don't see that character of softness and compassion that you normally see in a person who is connected to God. Instead you notice a harshness and an arrogance in them.

So what went wrong? Aren't they doing everything that we would expect from a religious person, like praying and giving charity? Why are they like this?

Religious life may start from a set of practices, but faith cannot be measured by these practices. Faith is to be accepted by people's minds and found in their hearts, and from there it moves naturally to the body and appears in their actions and deeds. It's not even something that should only remain in the mind. My mind can be a library full of books on theology, morality, and spirituality, but that is not enough; faith needs to come from the heart.

Faith is love

It is for this reason that Islamic teachings place great emphasis on achieving two goals in succession: to love God and to love for the sake of God.

To elaborate, it's important to note that faith is love. Faith is not a set of rituals or actions like praying and fasting.[8] Praying and fasting are very important, but they do not necessarily indicate piety and righteousness.[9] Both Imam

---

[8] This is not to underestimate ritual prayer (*salāt*) or fasting. They are very important. For example, Imam al-Baqir is quoted as saying, "The first thing that one will be questioned about is salāt. If it is accepted, other things will be accepted. And if it is rejected, other things will be rejected" (*Al-Kafi*, vol. 2, p. 268). However, the Qur'an and Sunnah have clearly indicated that there are conditions for the acceptability of rituals such as prayer and fasting. In a general way, the Qur'an says, "God only accepts from the pious" (5:27).

[9] For example, on how to discern a true believer, Imam Sadiq is quoted as saying:

> Do not pay attention to the lengthy bowing (*rukū'*) and prostration (*sujūd*) of a person, for these things may be performed simply out of habit, and were he to abandon these things, he would feel bad about it. Instead, pay attention to the truth of his speech and how he discharges trusts. (*Al-Kafi*, vol. 2, p. 106)

Also:

> Do not be deceived by their prayers and their fasting, for indeed, it often happens that a person prays and fasts (out of habit) so much so that if it is taken away from him, he feels especially uneasy. Rather, test them

13

Baqir and Imam Sadiq are quoted as saying: "Is faith anything other than love?"[10]

Faith is nothing but love. And pure love for God leads to loving others for the sake of God. Oftentimes, however, our love for God may not generate love for others. When our love for God is not genuine, and when it is rooted in our ego and selfish desires, we want to possess God and have a monopoly over Him, it cannot lead to loving others for the sake of God. But when our love for God is an outcome of understanding the beauty and greatness of God, anything that is associated with God (i.e., anything that is created by God) becomes an object of our love, by virtue of its connection to God.

Hadiths on loving for the sake of God

There are many hadiths about loving for the sake of God. I'll share a few of them with you. In one hadith, Prophet Muhammad says:

> By the One in whose hand my soul lies, you will never enter Heaven unless you have

---

with two things: truth in speech and discharging trusts. (Ibid., vol. 2, p. 104)

[10] For example, see *Bihar al-Anwar,* vol. 25, p. 97. The Arabic text is as follows:

هل الدين إلا الحُبّ ؟

14

faith, and you will never have faith unless
you love one another.[11]

Without love for others, it's impossible to enter Heaven.
The implication is that you cannot have faith if you don't
love each other. Heaven is a place where not only is God
loved, but everyone and everything there is loved.

Another hadith, which is found in many books, records a
conversation between God and Moses.[12] God asked Moses,
"What have you done for me?" to which Moses replied, "I
prayed, I fasted, and I gave alms." After listing the ways in
which Moses himself benefited from praying, fasting, and
giving alms, God said, "But what have you done for Me?"
Moses did not know that there could be something else to
offer to God. "(Please) show me the action that is carried
out (exclusively) for You!" he pleaded.

In parenthesis, if I want to do something for you, I cannot
impose what I want over you. It is for you to decide what
you want me to do for you.

In response to Moses' petition, God asked, "Have you ever
established relations (of *wilayah*) for My sake?" (*Wilayah* can

---

[11] *Mustadrak-u Wasa'il al-Shi'ah*, vol. 12, p. 222. The Arabic text is as
follows:

عَنِ النَّبِيِّ (ص) أَنَّهُ قَالَ : وَ الَّذِى نَفْسِى بِيَدِهِ لَا تَدْخُلُونَ الْجَنَّةَ حَتَّى تُؤْمِنُوا
وَ لَا تُؤْمِنُونَ حَتَّى تَحَابُّوا

[12] For example, it is recorded in *The Scale of Wisdom: A Compendium of Shi'a
Hadith*, compiled by M Muhammadi Rayshahri (vol. 1, p. 514 of the
Arabic edition).

be translated as "friendship," although it is much more than just friendship.) As an example, you may encounter someone who comes from another part of the world. This person doesn't look like you. He doesn't share your skin colour, nor does he speak the same language. Even though he barely has anything in common with you, you actively build a close relationship with him, just because of God.

The hadith ends with the following statement:

> It was then that Moses realized that the best of deeds is to love for the sake of God and to dislike for the sake of God.[13]

We can therefore conclude that if we truly love God, our love does not remain with God; our love will naturally be extended to anything that is connected to God. As I said in the previous round of Wings of Unity, everything is a creation of God. This means that everything is a sign of God and is therefore adorned with God's signature. If you look at anything, you can see the "face of God." In light of this, how can I truly love God and at the same time limit my love

---

[13] For example, see *Mustadrak-u Wasa'il al-Shi'ah*, vol. 12, p. 230. The Arabic text is as follows:

رُوِىَ أَنَّ اللَّهَ تَعَالَى قَالَ لِمُوسَى (ع): هَلْ عَمِلْتَ لِى عَمَلًا قَطُّ؟ قَالَ صَلَّيْتُ

لَكَ وَ صُمْتُ وَ تَصَدَّقْتُ. قَالَ اللَّهُ تَبَارَكَ وَ تَعَالَى لَهُ: أَمَّا الصَّلَاةُ فَلَكَ بُرْهَانٌ

وَ الصَّوْمُ جُنَّةٌ وَ الصَّدَقَةُ ظِلٌّ وَ الزَّكَاةُ نُورٌ فَأَىَّ عَمَلٍ عَمِلْتَ لِى؟ قَالَ مُوسَى

(ع): دُلَّنِى عَلَى الْعَمَلِ الَّذِى هُوَ لَكَ. قَالَ: يَا مُوسَى هَلْ وَالَيْتَ لِى وَلِيًّا؟

فَعَلِمَ مُوسَى أَنَّ أَفْضَلَ الْأَعْمَالِ الْحُبُّ فِى اللَّهِ وَ الْبُغْضُ فِى اللَّهِ.

to myself or at the most to my family, my community, and those who follow my religion? It's impossible! If God loves everything He creates, then our love should also extend to everything He created. Of course, there may be different degrees of love, but there must be no exclusion.

God's love is universal

We should try to imagine how God looks at people. This is no easy task. It's very difficult to imagine how God views His creation, but it can be instructive to at least make an effort. I think that when we advance in our spirituality, we are effectively moving away from the way people look at people and moving closer to the way God looks at people. In other words, the better you understand the way God looks at people, the closer you are to God. With my understanding of Islamic theology, spirituality, and philosophy, I cannot think of God as One who excludes or discriminates against any people based on their religion, gender, age, ethnicity, nationality, class, and so on.[14]

---

[14] However, as you may know, God may love some people more than others on the basis of their moral merits and the efforts put forth towards their spiritual betterment and the betterment of other people's lives. That is to say, the virtuous and the vicious are not on equal footing. The Qur'an says:

> Shall We treat those who have faith and do righteous deeds like those who cause corruption on earth? Shall We treat the Godwary like the vicious? (38:28)

God's love is undivided

There is a beautiful divine saying[15] in which God says, "I love each of you and pay attention to each of you as if you are My only servant, but you treat Me as if you have many lords."[16] Meaning, even if there was no other human being in the entire world, God would not have loved me more than He does now. It's not that there are so many people in the world that God needs to divide His love between billions of us. On the contrary, He loves each one of us as if He has no other person to love.

When you pray to God, you should not think that since there are so many others who are also praying to Him, He is therefore only partially attentive. Indeed, God is fully there for everyone; His undivided attention and love are directed at us in a way where it is as if He has nothing else to do.

Our love for God must be complete and pure

Unfortunately, we don't give one hundred percent of our attention and one hundred percent of our love to God. We divide it, leaving only part of it for God, and that is completely unfair. If God gives His infinite love and

---

We also know that God does not endorse criminal acts or vicious qualities and habits. However, there is nothing that exists unless it is embraced by God's mercy.

[15] A divine saying (or *hadith qudsi*) is a non-scriptural, direct quote from God as said through some of the prophets.

[16] This hadith is wide-spread orally, but I have not yet been able to find the reference for it in early collections of hadith.

attention to each one of us, we should at least give all of our *limited* heart and attention to Him. It's not a matter of how big our heart is. The important thing is that we give all of it to God. A person's heart can be very small, but what matters most is that it's pure. To give an analogy, when you offer someone a glass of water, what matters most is not the quantity of the water but that the water is pure.

Pure love is most precious to God. This universe, with all its stars and galaxies, cannot contain God.[17] But a pure heart, even if it's the heart of a child, can be a place where God comes and settles. If we can give our pure heart to God, He will accept it and enter it. And when our heart is overcome by God, it becomes a Godly heart that loves everyone.

How our love for God leads to and gives orientation to our love for others

After this stage, a process of introspection begins. Now that you are consumed by God's love, you want to love everyone for the sake of God. But you don't know how to do it; you are not used to feeling this way. You start to ask questions that may never have occurred to you had you not gone through this experience. Questions like, "How much should I love my family?" "How much should I love my

---

[17] *Bihar al-Anwar*, vol. 55, p. 39. The text of the hadith is as follows:

فِى الْحَدِيثِ الْقُدْسِىِّ: لَمْ يَسَعْنِى سَمَائِى وَلَا أَرْضِى وَ وَسِعَنِى قَلْبُ عَبْدِى

الْمُؤْمِنِ

Neither my sky nor my earth contained Me, but the heart of my faithful servant contained Me.

community?" "How much should I love people of other faiths?"

I think that this last question is one of the most difficult questions. If I want to give my heart to God, how should I relate to people of other religions? It's a difficult question because we have been brought up and educated to think, "My religion is divine," "My religion is the most loved religion by God," or (for some people), "My religion is the *only* religion that is loved by God." At the very least, some people will say that those who belong to their religion are the most loved by God.

It's quite challenging to reach the point where on the one hand, you are faithful to your religion – to the extent that you are ready to die for your faith – and on the other hand, you have so much love for God that through God you tend to love everyone.

Expanding oneself to include others
We have to go through many challenges in order to refine and purify ourselves. For example, marriage can be one way of getting rid of the ego. Before marriage, people are usually inclined to think only about themselves. After marriage, however, at least if it's a successful marriage, I learn that it's not only about me; I now have a spouse, children, and in-laws. So marriage can be a step towards uniting with other people.

In addition to my family, I have to consider my community. It's not only my family, my parents, and my cousins; it's all adherents of my religion – all those who go to the mosque or to the church. They are also part of my family. So now I have an extended family in the form of my community.

Then we continue to stretch the family until it includes all believers and all nations. The idea is that we must try to get rid of anything that can act as a partition or a barrier.

Religion: a path towards God, not a barrier

It seems that as we go through this process of removing barriers, there is something at the very end that perhaps rarely anyone has been able to get rid of, and that is our attachment to our religion. This is because we have always looked at our religion as the "front view" of God, which makes it difficult for us to look at God and humanity without using the lens of our religion.

Again, I repeat: I am ready to die for my religion, and I hope I am honest in making this claim. And when I say that religion may become a barrier, I don't mean to underestimate my religion; religion is meant to take us towards God. But a point may come when you want to gain a Godly vision and see how God views your religion and other religions. Of course, this by itself can be a new religion, but not new in the sense that you are adding to the number of religions in the world; rather, it's a new way of understanding religions, or a new way of life.

The following example may help. At night, the moon and stars reflect light. When there is a full moon, more light is reflected. But where does this light come from? It doesn't come from the moon or the stars. It comes from the sun. In this analogy, let's say that the moon is your religion, if your religion happens to be the best religion. Now, I may be satisfied with the light of a single star. Meanwhile there is a whole moon I'm missing out on. But even if you follow the best religion – the most pleasing one to God – at best you are illuminated by the moon. This is while there are people who are satisfied with stars, and others who just look down and don't even look at the moon or the stars though they may benefit from their light. Likewise, no one can deny that everyone in the world is benefiting from the legacy of prophets and religions, even if they are not religious people.

At night, beams of light radiate from the sun and reach us through the moon and stars. But when the day comes, the sun also comes out, causing the moon and stars to disappear. Now that it is day time, you only see the sun. As long as the sun is shining, neither does the moon try to compete with the sun, nor does any person with vision feel the need to search for the moon or stars. Everything is bright and clear.

On the Day of Judgment there won't be any test or need to choose a certain religion. Everyone will understand and admit the truth. The Qur'an says that on the Day of Judgment people will be asked, "To whom belongs the kingdom today?" to which everyone – religious or not – will respond, "To God, the One, the all-Paramount!"[18]

---

[18] Qur'an 40:16. The Arabic text is as follows:

لِمَنِ المُلْك اليَوْم لله الواحد القَهَّار

22

In this world, we definitely need religion. But on that day there will be no need for religion; everything will be crystal clear. As you move towards God, your understanding of religion changes and enables you to reach a point where you can look at everything in the way that God sees things – but as much as is humanly possible. We are finite, which means we can never understand the world exactly as God understands it. Nonetheless, we can certainly try to get closer and closer to that point.

Thus, in this world, there will always be religions, but this does not mean that we should let our understanding of our religion limit us. A good religion is the one that, when understood properly, opens your eyes, expands your vision, and helps you get closer to having a Godly vision.

Let me put it another way. Is God Jewish, Christian, or Muslim? The Qur'an speaks of a debate that took place over which religion Abraham belonged to. There were Jews who claimed that Abraham was a Jew, and there were Christians who claimed that he was a Christian. Perhaps not every Jew and Christian made this claim; the Qur'an speaks of a group of Jews and Christians who lived in the Arabian Peninsula at the time. Drawing the debate to a close, God says:

> Abraham was neither a Jew nor a Christian.
> Rather he was a *hanif* (inclining towards

truth), a *muslim* (submissive to God), and he
was not one of the polytheists.[19]

Abraham refused to be defined by any labels. He was simply
someone who was submissive to God. We believe that
Prophet Muhammad also did the same. Prophet Muhammad
did not want to be called, "The Founder of the
Muhammadian[20] Religion" or labeled in some other way. He
did not want to be the founder of any religion; he simply
wanted to call people once again towards God, just as
Abraham called people towards God. He called people to
submit themselves to the Absolute Truth and not to allow
any label – be it a religious or denominational title – to limit
them.

Religion should help us to relate to and care for each other

If we have a proper religion, and we also understand it
properly, it should help us relate to other people – including
other religious communities – and as much as possible try to
look at them the way God looks at them. Let me give you an
example. Take the following scenario: You are a Christian
priest who accepts donations from the Christian
congregation – donations which are meant to be used for a

---

[19] Qur'an 3:67. The Arabic text is as follows:

$$\text{ما كانَ إبْراهيمُ يَهودِيّا وَلا نَصْرانِيّا ولكِن كانَ حَنيفا مُسْلِما وَما كانَ مِنَ المُشْرِكين}$$

[20] In fact, Muslims have been highly critical of orientalist writers'
invention of the term "Muhammadanism" to refer to Islam.

24

Christian cause. The fact that they are not general donations is an important detail in this scenario; those who donated explicitly stated that the money must be used for a "Christian cause." Let's say the Muslims in your area do not have a place to worship God (i.e., they don't have a mosque to go to). Bearing in mind what donors have stipulated, what would you do in this case? Would you consider it a Christian cause to help Muslims educate their children or even build a mosque in order to pray to God? Or would you say, "We can't spend the money. It's not a Christian cause." This may appear to be an easy question but it's actually a tough one.

And in my case, if I'm given some money and asked to use it for a project that is Islamic, can this Islamic project include helping people of another faith pray to God?

I think that if my understanding of Christianity or Islam is right, the answer would be a resounding yes. But if my Islam and Christianity are not true Islam and true Christianity, I would most likely say, "No, helping people to pray to God in an Islamic way is the only way that I can consider it as an Islamic project," or, "Praying to God in a Christian way is the only way I can consider this to be a Christian project."

If I've understood Islam in a way that God wants me to understand Islam, in *my* religion I should be encouraged to help other religious communities. It's no longer Islam versus other religions; there should be a place for other religions in *my* Islam, if it's a Godly Islam. So instead of striving to establish dialogue between Islam and (for example) Christianity, I hope I would be given a kind of understanding of Islam in which people of other faiths are present, because this is the only way I can understand Islam as being pleasing to God.

For example, in Islam we have the concept of being *khalifatullah,* or "the vicegerent of God." We believe that Adam was a vicegerent of God, David was a vicegerent of God, Imam Mahdi is a vicegerent of God, and so on. So how will a person who is a vicegerent or representative of God on earth act? He will not act according to a limited version of Islam. He will act according to an expanded version of Islam because it has to be aligned with the way God wants to run this world, and God is the Lord of everyone.

We, too, have to understand how our understanding of our religion can broaden our vision and not limit our vision, and how it can broaden our heart and not limit our heart. The moment you reach the point where you consider it your religious duty to support other religions, to love other religious communities, to do your best for them, and to sacrifice for them, I think that is when you have reached that expanded version of your religion. At that stage you will begin to see that the difference between you and people from other faiths who have also reached this is minuscule.

How must identity be understood today?

It was in Palermo when I first shared a reflection I had about identity, and I would also like to share it with you.[21] Our religious identity is very important to us, but in the past, I think that for the most part our understanding of our religious identity was unenlightened, or at least it was not enlightened in a way that suits today's world. Imagine that both Christians and Muslims live in a village or town and a child or student comes to the church and you want to make sure that they develop a good sense of identity. How would you explain what it means to be a Christian in this village where there are Muslims and Christians living together? How would you educate them about their identity? You might say, "Don't do anything that Muslims do. Be very careful; don't get too close to them. Don't do what they do and you're on the safe side." This way of trying to help someone preserve their identity was far easier than to explain what it means to be Christian. Instead of giving them catechism and teaching many things, the easiest thing for them was just to be separate from Muslims and for Muslims just to be separate from Christians. This how they were able to understand their identity.

Maybe in a place like Northern Ireland, being either Catholic or Protestant was the main thing in the world for them. The main thing for Catholics was simply not to be like

---

[21] This idea was presented in the opening session of the 28th Congress of European Professors of Islamic and Arabic Studies on September 12, 2016. The theme of the Congress was "Islam & Mediterranean: Identity, Alterity & Interactions."

Protestants and maybe for Protestants not to be like Catholics. Maybe among Sunni and Shi'a in some places it's also like this.

So a great part – not the only part, but a great part – of your understanding of identity used to come from what you are *not* much more than what you *are* or what you are supposed to be. This idea that a Muslim is someone who is not a Christian is deeply built in some people's minds and hearts. It's the idea that a Muslim is not just the one who goes to the mosque, but a Muslim is the one who does not go to the church.

These two come hand-in-hand. If you are a Muslim you don't go to church, and if you are a Christian you don't go to the mosque. This has been built as part of our understanding of identity. If you are a Muslim, your friends should be Muslims. If you are Christian, your friends should be Christians.

I think the world in which we live is so interconnected – across religions and across cultures – that you can no longer have this type of understanding about your identity. You have to build on your own constructive understanding of identity and you also have a clear understanding of how to reach out. You can no longer build your identity just by saying what you are not. You have to work hard to give today's Muslim a clear understanding of what it means to be a Muslim and what it means to have a Muslim life, a Muslim personality, and a Muslim character. And part of it is: how, as a Muslim, you should relate to people of other faiths, how you should love them, and how you should try to serve them. It's a big shift in understanding identity, and until it's achieved, we may go through a stage where either people don't have a clear understanding of identity or they are very rigid. Either they are confused and don't know what it means to be a Muslim who is not rigid, or they are very exclusive and regard others as having diluted their faith.

So I think that we need to prepare ourselves for a new era in which religions, at least religions with a divine origin (i.e. Abrahamic origins), will not look at each other as rivals and competitors; an era in which religious leaders feel responsible not only for their own community but for other faith communities.

If today God wanted to choose someone – and this is a question I've thought about often – what would that person be like? Imagine that there was a way to ask God, "O God, please choose someone from among us to be Your vicegerent (Your representative), someone who can take care of all of us," what would that person's character be like? What type of Muslim or Christian or Jew or person of any other faith would God choose to take care of all of humanity? A man of God should be someone who cares about everyone; someone who cares for all religious communities and helps them move towards God.

Love for the sake of God purifies one's heart and leads to complete attachment to God

So love for the sake of God is a purifying factor and it can get to the stage where you get rid of all attachments and affiliations; you get rid of anything that is not one hundred percent Godly.

There is a beautiful supplication (i.e., *du'a*) that Imam Khomeini would often end his lectures with in the seminary. It's called *Munajaat al-Sha'baaniyyah*. It's a whispered prayer that we are told was recited by all of our Imams. Allow me to quote a passage from it:

> My Lord, (please) connect me to the most brilliant light of Your dignity so that I will recognize You and leave all else.[22]

Here the supplicant is essentially saying, "Please enable me to join (and reach) the light of Your dignity – which is the type of light that brings the most joy – so that I can know You and become completely detached from anything other than You."

You are moving towards the source of light. In the process of moving towards the Absolute Light, it becomes necessary to penetrate through many barriers. Imagine that there are one hundred curtains, and the light of God is so powerful that it can radiate through that many curtains. But you don't settle for this amount of light; you want to remove these curtains. You will not be satisfied until you reach the Source. This is where there is only you and God, with nothing to come in between.

---

[22] The Arabic text is as follows:

إلهى وَٱلْحِقْنى بِنور عِزِّك الأَبْهَج فَأَكُون لَكَ عارِفاً وَعَن سِواكَ مُنْحَرِفاً

Another passage from the same whispered prayer reads thus:

> My Lord, (please) grant me absolute devotion to You, and illuminate the sights of our hearts with the light of looking at You, so that the sights of the hearts will penetrate the screens of light, and arrives at the core of Your Magnificence.[23]

We have to work hard to reach this state across different dimensions of our lives; in our personal life, family life, community life, political life, economic life, theological life, and so on. In everything we do, we have to make sure that we keep moving towards God. The more we move towards God, the more humble become, which will in turn broaden our vision and our hearts.

This is what I wanted to share with you today, and I'm sorry if I was not clear enough. Thank you.

---

[23] The Arabic text is as follows:

إلهى هَبْ لى كَمال الإنْقِطاع إلَيكَ وأنِر أبْصارَ قُلوبِنا بِضياءِ نَظَرِها إلَيْكَ
حَتّى تَخرِقَ أبْصار القُلوب حُجُب النّور فَتَصِلَ إلى مَعْدِن الْعَظَمَة

Comments and Reflections[1] [2]

Piero: I'm very happy about this lecture. Very, very happy. There are many things to share. I'd like to start with the image of the sun, the moon, and the stars that you used: God is the sun, the source of the light, and we should not get confused and think that the light of the moon and the stars comes from themselves; their light comes from the sun. Chiara uses this image to describe her experience of God, that when the sun comes, the moon and the stars go away. She says that first she used to refer to and look at the moon, who is represented by Mary in the Christian tradition, and the stars, which are the saints, or we can say the prophets. She talks about the Christian saints, but I think she actually means the saints of all religions. In fact when she used to meet men of God, like the Buddhist etc., she would say that she could feel the presence of God. Therefore, she would not make a distinction among the saints, even if they were followers of other religions or Christian denominations.

---

[1] This section comprises a collection of comments made by participants, including Dr. Shomali, immediately following his presentation. Some of the comments were originally made in Italian and subsequently translated into English by Ms. Hanieh Tarkian.

[2] Please note that the comments below are taken from the transcript of the session and need to be checked and verified by those who have made them.

But the light comes from the sun, and she also says that at noon, the sun's light illuminates everything, causing the stars and the moon to disappear. So they are the sun, but at the same time they are something different from the sun.

She also says that to see God as the source of light has changed her perspective on religion. First she used to look at Jesus, as he is the Word of God who came to the earth, but now she looks at God and Jesus is at His side, which is something very powerful for a Christian to say, but yet normal. In fact, you mentioned that hadith about God and his servant; when Jesus was baptised, the sky opened up and a voice said, "You are my servant." We, all of us, are servants and sons of God, and God is the Father. So for Chiara, this was a different experience. It doesn't mean to put aside the Christian view, but to look at it from a new point of view. This is very close to what you said. I think this experience was crucial for Chiara, especially when she wanted to have dialogue with people of other religions.

Another point I was affected by was this: you started by mentioning atheism and asking how we can "communicate" and "give" God, and you made a very deep and truthful analysis. God can be communicated only when He Himself communicates Himself; I can communicate Him to others only if He possesses me completely, and this is very important. It is the root of everything. I remember when Chiara used to say that you can communicate God to others only when you are completely possessed by Him and in Him. Otherwise you are not communicating God, but rather communicating the image of God that is in your mind. So I think we can agree with what you said. In the Christian faith, this is linked to the reality of Jesus, which Chiara highlights in her concept of "Jesus abandoned": Jesus realizes his plan when he experiences complete detachment; out of love for others he experiences the test and the pain of the crucifixion, etc. He is the master of faith in God. Jesus abandoned experiences emptiness from God because of love, and this is faith. What is faith? Jesus abandoned is faith – complete faith in God – which corresponds to love for the other. I think this faith in God is the eye of the needle through which, as the Gospel says, our religious life should pass. So for us Christians, it should pass by Jesus abandoned. This is how we label it, but it corresponds to what you said, just from another point of view.

Saint Paul in the Gospel says that although Jesus was one with God, he did not consider Him to be his own treasure. So he annihilated himself, and this is why God glorified him. This is fundamental. This concept of Jesus abandoned was not understood over two thousand years of Christian history. In fact when Chiara started to talk about this concept, the bishop of Trento said that this is an unknown doctrine in Christianity and you should not talk about it. Chiara replied, "You are the religious authority so I will obey you," and she told her sisters not to talk about Jesus abandoned anymore, as not talking about it anymore is actually living it. The highest love is not talking anymore about what is our highest love. When the bishop came to know this, he called Chiara and told her, "Even if I still tell you not to talk about it, please talk about it!"

35

This concept of Jesus abandoned is still a big mystery in the Christian church.

Faith in Jesus detached the Hebrew identity from religion, so it was no longer necessary to be of the Hebrew people to be religious, and therefore even non-Hebrew people could have faith in God. In the beginning there was a big conflict concerning this within the Christian church.

Saint Paul said, "I make myself everything for everyone, as Jesus made himself everything for everyone: Hebrew with the Hebrews, pagan with the pagans," because he learned universality from Jesus. Then again at certain points in history there was a restriction but now... What you are saying is something extraordinary. I have never heard it from a follower of another religion, and it would even be challenging for me to say it myself.

About how God looks at the world and looks at everyone— God looks at everyone like they are His only servant. In his book *Spiritual Exercises*, Ignatius of Loyola says that the first thing you should do is imagine how God looks at the world, as you said; God looks at everyone and loves everyone, and He sends Jesus and you are called to reply to that love. Chiara says that this look of God that you acquire is the look that Jesus lived in his abandonment. God is detached from Himself, and in order to be in God, you should be detached from everything that is not God. This is because God Himself is detached from Himself in His love, and this is His sanctity, His light. He is pure light and pure love. The eye with which God looks at the world is the same with which

Jesus looks, but the pupil of this eye is the abandonment. You should empty yourself from everything to go towards God. Your detachment is a reply to His detachment, this pupil through which He looks at the world.

The last thing I want to say is that my "I" cannot go towards God if He doesn't embrace everyone else. I'm not only called to love everyone in God, but I also cannot go towards God if I exclude even a single person. Chiara says, "My 'I' is humanity. I can embrace everyone." With this understanding, every religion has its own identity, there is not syncretism, but it detaches from itself and can bring people towards God. We Christians can clearly see this in our Pope Francis, who chose this name because he experiences poverty and detachment from everything while also embracing everyone. This is why he is often criticized, even within the Church itself. Some people say that he is destroying the Christian identity because he doesn't differentiate among people and is open to other religions. I think this is a sign of this time. As you said, we are working for a new era.

I don't see any contrast between what I said this morning and what you said, so why don't we publish a book with these ideas? Of course developed and redefined. A book in English and Italian.

Sharzad: The interesting thing is that all of us are actually radical believers in our religions. This is something exceptional to meet in unity. We are faithful to our own religious identities. Our main identity is the human identity which is not detached from the divine identity, as the Qur'an says: the divine spirit was blown into the human being. Into every human being, believer or not. So every human being is also divine; the true and essential identity of each human being is human, which is at the same time divine. The religious identity is not the essential one; it is accidental. The Qur'an confirms what you two said. The word *noor* (i.e., light) is never plural. If we are in the light, we are in unity. On the other hand the word "darkness" is always plural, since it cannot reach unity.

About the concept of emptiness, even if there is no concept of the son in Islam, the servant is the one who has emptied himself and exists in the love of God, in complete unity – empty of what prevents him from unity. The servant still remains, but he is full of unity.

Professor Shomali mentioned an attitude among Muslims. Some are arrogant; they judge others and feel superior, which I have also seen in the Christian world. This is religious pride: we think we possess the truth. I think what we are experiencing today goes beyond everything. It guides us towards the light, so our religions become light and not a limit, and in this way we can help our own societies.

Dr. Shomali: I would like to refer to some verses of the Qur'an that I think need more attention; in my own reflection I want to work more on these verses.

If you remember, we spoke about the concept of the "Face of God" in the previous round of Wings of Unity. It was also very interesting for me that Pope Francis later, in a letter to the sisters, talked about them seeking the "Face of God." So it's a very important concept for us.

Among the verses in the Qur'an that relate to the "Face of God," there are a few verses that talk about submitting your face to God. One example is the following:

> Certainly whoever submits his face to God and is virtuous, he shall have his reward near his Lord, and they shall have no fear, nor shall they grieve. (Qur'an 2:112)[3]

The last part about having no reason to fear and having no grief is a very important expression that is sometimes repeated in the Qur'an in reference to those who are very close to God; we call them *awliyaa'ullah*, the friends of God. If you want to be a friend of God, then what you need to do is submit your face to God and do good things.

In another verse, God says to the Prophet:

> So if they argue with you (O Prophet), say, "I have submitted my face to God, and [so has] he who follows me." (Qur'an 3:20)[4]

---

[3] The Arabic text is as follows:

بلى مَن أَسْلَمَ وَجْهَهُ لِلَّه وهُو مُحسِن فَلَهُ أجرُهُ عِندَ رَبِّهِ ولا خَوف عَلَيهِم
ولا هُم يَحزَنون

[4] The Arabic text is as follows:

فإن حاجّوكَ فَقُل أسلَمتُ وَجهِيَ لِلّهِ وَمَنِ اتَّبَعَن

"If they debate with you" about which religion or way of life is true, tell them, "I and whoever follows me have submitted our faces to God." You don't need to say anything else; it's all-encompassing.

In another verse, God goes further:

> And who has a better religion than him who submits his face to God, being virtuous, and follows the creed of Abraham, a *hanif*? And God took Abraham for a dedicated friend. (Qur'an 4:125)[5]

"Who has a better religion than he who submits his face to God, does good things, and follows the path of Abraham who was moving towards Truth?" *Hanif* means someone who deviates from falsehood and moves towards the truth. "—And God chose Abraham as His friend." So if you want to be a friend of God, follow the path of Abraham and that is to submit your face to God and do good things. You cannot really submit your face to God and do nothing or do bad things; you must do good things.

Elsewhere the Qur'an says:

---

[5] The Arabic text is as follows:

وَمَن أَحسَنُ دِينا مِّمَّن أَسلَمَ وَجهَهُ لِلَّه وَهُوَ مُحسِن وَاتَّبَعَ مِلَّة إِبراهِيمَ حَنِيفا

واتخذَ اللهُ إِبراهِيمَ خَلِيلا

40

Whoever surrenders his face to God and is virtuous, has certainly held fast to the firmest handle, and with God lies the outcome of all matters. (Qur'an 31:22)[6]

This shows that what I try to declare is deeply rooted in the Qur'an, that at the end of the day, you choose a direction, which is God, submit your face to Him, and do good things. This is the core of all Abrahamic religions and possibly other religions as well but we are speaking now about Abrahamic religions.

Here you don't see a big difference. As I said yesterday, I think that submission to God – or submitting your face to God – constitutes ninety-nine percent of faith, while doing good deeds constitutes one percent. Submission is a condition of heart, but doing good actions is a condition of bodily organs. Submission is about one's direction is life and that is the main thing to be concerned about. Unfortunately, we spend ninety-nine or one hundred percent of our attention on what we do as religious practices, and in the process we neglect the main thing, which is to submit ourselves to God wholeheartedly.

I myself wanted to reflect on these verses but I thought to also share them with you.

---

[6] The Arabic text is as follows:

وَمَن يُسْلِمْ وَجْهَهُ إِلَى اللهِ وَهُوَ مُحْسِنٌ فَقَدِ اسْتَمْسَكَ بِالْعُرْوَةِ الْوُثْقَى وَإِلَى اللهِ عَاقِبَةُ الْأُمُورِ

Another point is that in some verses it says *aslama wajhahu lillaah*, while in others it says *aslama wajhahu ilallah*. I think this refers to two stages: one is to submit your face *to* God, meaning you are moving, and the other is submitting your face *for* God, meaning you have an encounter with God.

If you are on a plane that is moving fast on the runway, at that point you are not facing your destination; instead, you are just moving in that direction. But when it reaches the point where it detaches itself from the earth and you go up to the sky, then you can have an encounter with the sun, for example. Believers first have to move towards God, but then you reach the point where you face God. It seems this might be the difference between the two verses: moving towards that encounter and already facing God.

Farha: I'll say that today was amazing and I enjoyed everything. There were many questions in my mind which are (now) clear to me. It is like I don't need to do my PhD; I got the answers. Especially Professor Shomali, your first session and now (in this session). You know, I also used to think along similar lines but I always had a doubt about whether I'm thinking in the right way. Sometimes I thought I'm becoming too pessimistic. Maybe I'm merging things; because the situation is like this so maybe I was thinking these might be the possibilities but this is not actually the possibility. (I thought) I'm just thinking about things in a different way but they are not like this. But now, after listening to you, I think that there are people who also think maybe in a crazy way but in a right direction. So I'm feeling more confident and very clear. I'm very happy. Thanks a lot.

And you know, I used to think that because there's one God then of course there will be one humanity, and then I used to think, "Why do people not understand this?" There are so many good philosophers, theologians, and experts—why is it that this small thing has not come to their minds? Well of course it was in their mind and it is in their mind, but they are in very limited numbers.

But I also think that everything has a situation point, and I think now humanity is at the maturation point that now we can see that these differences are not just differences but they have negative things along with it. So we need to clear the air and see clearly; we need to take out these layers and see the right thing.

So I think now this is the time when humanity is becoming more mature, and I think meetings like this are a kind of step in that direction. And I think now people are becoming ready to understand things because maybe they are also sick of what is going on.

Attendee: Both talks were wonderful. I could see the link between both of them and it made me contemplate many points. Now I'm going to be left thinking and going through a lot of points, such as how to lose yourself in God, and how to make space for God, and what are those core qualities that allow us to make that space for God. Is it truthfulness? Humbleness? What are those qualities? Do we share those qualities in Christianity and Islam? And how do we implement them and include them in our educational system as well? How do we teach our teenagers from a young age, and how do we please God so that He makes Himself among us as you said? And how to find ourselves one in God, how do we love God and extend that to other people, and how much have religious people been affected by secularism? So it just left me thinking about these points.

And then Dr. Shomali's points as well, when God says, "I love each of you as if you are My only servant," I'm wondering if we have to struggle to really think about that or if we get that right away. Because I think perhaps that is a struggle to think of God as loving each one of us as if we are His only servant. Perhaps we think in terms of God making so many comparisons. And another interesting point is also when Dr. Shomali said that the end point to get rid of our ego is to get rid of that attachment to religion. What's interesting is that that's the end point instead of a beginning point or middle point. But that end point was very profound; that was a very new idea.

All in all I pray that God gives us the blessing of sincerity amongst each other and in our intentions and works, that we're able to implement all of this. I'm interested to know all of the practical aspects to it so that we can do it in the most efficient way in our society.

Paolo: I was joking during the break with Mohammad, telling him that for Thursday evening and the Q&A that we had with both of you, we gave the title, The *Frontiers of Interreligious Dialogue*. I was telling him that probably beyond the frontiers of interreligious dialogue, we need to get rid of our religions. Sometimes it seems to me that our baggage that we bring around the table of dialogue is so strong that our being religious is kind of an obstacle to really being able to open ourselves and expose ourselves in the way that Piero and Mohammad did today, being free to say something that can be not dangerous for our life per se, but for our identity; our being like a hole. So sometimes we open ourselves in a way that only the other one or God through the other one can keep us on our feet. I think that this is a strong and very deep space where we can re-find ourselves and our religions in a way that is beyond the frontiers that we had today. So thank you very much.

Mariella: When I heard that the meeting was confirmed for this date, there was a moment in my heart, like, my heart jumped because my first meeting of Wings of Unity was a transforming meeting, I felt not only the presence of God but I felt God at work within us.

It was not only a transforming experience the first time that we were together, but it was the presence of God starting a new era because (He has) completely chosen some instruments, some people who want to bring His presence in a new way. So my heart jumped because I said, "God, what are you preparing in these coming days for us?" And when God is at work, anything can happen; we should be prepared not only for a revolution, but to be in front of "The Sun."

When you were talking—it started already last Thursday when you came and you spoke to the community during the cultural night about what interreligious dialogue means for you. There I felt, and I touched with my hands, because I

45

was in the back and I could see the reaction of people, that what you were sharing as an experience was already becoming a reality among us. So I said, "This is only the introduction and I'm preparing myself for the next days." But at the same time, I said, "To be able to be this container of this grace, of this light, I should not expect anything." So I said, "I want to go like a book that has white pages, where You can write anything. Or a container that doesn't have anything, where You can place whatever You have planned for us."

And to tell you the truth, today, at a certain point I could no longer distinguish between who represents the Islamic religion and who represents the Christian, Catholic tradition. So I said, "I had a little foretaste of that experience of Paradise," because I thought there, there will be no distinction anymore. There, we will love one another and there, we will understand completely. So this is an experience that is for humanity, as you have shared in a marvellous way today.

Now again my heart jumps and I say, "How do we bring this outside?" Now You transformed us into a new reality. We are no longer the same people when I came in this morning; surely, we are no longer the same. So now You have to tell us *how* to bring it with words, with life, with gesture, with experience. Now You guide us on what is the next step, because the world needs this.

My heart is overflowing with thanksgiving to God for this experience, but also for each one of you, because each one of you has been this instrument of God to make it possible. And we thank Chiara also who made this reality a tangible experience. The more I understood today the experience with Chiara and Igino Giordani, the reason and the step of what happened in that unity that is discovered, and at the same time as I go ahead, I feel that I don't understand it completely. The more I go ahead, there is the awareness that I know too little about it. This is the awareness in our journey together. So I don't say it's a transforming experience; it's a total changing perspective of life, of being a child of God, and I surrender myself together with all of you to whatever God wants from us. Surely there is not only great hope, but there is the certainty that unity is possible because today we have touched it with our hearts, with our soul, and with our minds.

Roberto: Can I say something? I'm sorry that I missed your presentation, Mohammad, but from whatever feedback was given, I could perceive at least moving, inspirational vibrations of the deep spiritual dimension of your presentation.

I just wanted to support an idea that Piero came out with. It is the idea of having a small publication of the present seminar but also adding something more to it. I also want to support it with a feeling that I had when I came back from a visit to your seminary in London. So many people asked me why I went to London. When I explained to them that I was invited to speak in a Shi'a seminary to Shi'a men and women, I had all sorts of reactions. You understand well that in Europe in this moment there are so many feelings on one side and the other, and the idea that a Catholic Italian would go to speak – along with another Italian, because Paolo and I went together – in a seminary of Shi'a Muslims in London, was a witness by itself. In a way it is sometimes a bit devastating for those who think in traditional, ultra-orthodox ways, both within the Catholic fold and also among people who have no interest in religion at the moment.

So I feel that we have to also give a sign outside of this wonderful experience that we have among ourselves, and a sign can be given in a way obviously to our own personal experiences which we carry within ourselves, for the very fact that we are being together and are being transformed by our being together, and probably also at the academic level, but not only at the academic level. Also I would say in the educational field, meaning signs of the presence of something new. It may be something very small. It may be a booklet with your papers and presentations, but also personal experiences like inviting Catholics to speak to pupils and scholars in a Muslim seminary, and you coming to Loppiano and addressing a large Catholic crowd about Islam...

So I would strongly encourage, in a simple way, for us to start with something where we put together something of the previous seminar last July, something of this seminar, and something from previous experiences about working together. People in Europe, people within the Catholic Church, people within Islam, need concrete signs that dialogue is possible, and we can give not only a witness that it is possible, but we can also think together. We propose this to other people because we are already beyond the frontiers of that. So this is my proposal to support what Piero said...

Piero: Even if it was only a day, I feel like I have crossed a big sea. I see that everyone is happy. What do you think, Rita?

Rita: I think we should elaborate on it, since it can lead to misinterpretations, even if it is a deep experience.

Piero: This is why I had said that we should elaborate on this with more attention. I think we should give the responsibility of this to Sofia Global Studies.

Bennie: I had two feelings. The first Wings (of Unity) was such a strong experience that I said, "What will God let us live now?" And now that we are at the end of the day, we know it; it was able to surprise us.

I think that the two other days were also important. To feel that what we lived in a small circle is part of Loppiano, is really part of Loppiano, and it was very important that the city could make the experience. I briefed the assembly of the Focolare in Loppiano about our experience on Sunday, very briefly, but I desire that they would really have location [presence?] and this was very happy thing because we need the sustainment of the broader community.

Then yesterday, I think the afternoon was important. I was not there the entire time but to feel that, when some people who are less prepared come forward with some less easy points, it is not harming anything. There is something else we are already living, so this is history. It's life. We will have to struggle with some things but it doesn't spoil the atmosphere. I was very happy about that. You'll always have people more or less prepared. I think today there were many things. Obviously, what we shared yesterday is very lived, and as you say this is the martyrdom of our times. It's a martyrdom we take together. I'm very aware that these are serious things, but God also gives us the capacity to live them in a very simple way. So that seems to be so well-balanced.

It was also very important to have the presence of Rita. I'm very happy about so many things and I think that Wings of Unity is a kind of first son or first daughter of Sophia Global Studies. There is something that also gives light on the other; this is very special, and this is also thanks to, sure, a long history: twenty years. But God prepares well.

Piero: Maybe we can consider this not the end of dialogue but the beginning of a new form or structure of dialogue. Think together and walk together in God. As Pope Francis says, unity is not the final destination but it is a walk. We should focus on this. My suggestion is for the Islamic Center and Sophia Global Studies to collaborate on a project and see how we can develop this, in both Italian and English. We should think about whether to create one booklet or two, one in England and one in Italy, with an introduction that narrates our experiences. Maybe Roberto can work on it.

The second important thing that was stressed is the importance of living all of this and how to live it. During the summer school we should not teach notions, even if the youth need to be more familiar with each other, since maybe the young Christians don't know much about Islam or the young Muslims don't know much about Christianity. We need to communicate our experience of life to them and give them the "keys" of life, each within his or her own religion, but with the open-mindedness that we mentioned. It is clear that we should not limit ourselves to something abstract: know each other to know God and to meet God.

This can become a new paradigm for us in our religions, for our time. It can become a very important experience. We will talk about that tomorrow.

A third thing is that in October, we will celebrate the ten-year anniversary of Sophia University along with the new academic year, and we will also inaugurate Sophia Global Studies. It is important that Dr. Shomali attends this inauguration. It could be an opportunity to introduce our experience, to meet other people, and to also see how we can continue this project – this walk of Sophia Global Studies.

So these are three things to work on.

Today, we at Sophia announce that dialogue is over. Sophia has now been running for ten years. I think that it is now time to change, because when things are doing well it is time to change them, otherwise they become old.

Among Brothers and Sisters
of Different Faiths[1]

Hujjatul Islam Dr Mohammad Ali Shomali answers a number of important questions posed by students at the Sophia University Institute during his last visit to Italy

Hujjatul Islam Dr Mohammad Ali Shomali – director of the Islamic Centre of England – together with some members of the Hawza Ilmiyya (Islamic Seminary) of England, visited Sophia University Institute in Loppiano, Italy, 12th to 14th January 2017.

His visit represents one of many ongoing encounters between Shi'a Muslims and members of the Focolare Movement – a grassroots Catholic organisation based in Italy with a presence in many countries across the world. The dialogue between the two groups, which began more than 19 years ago, has recently focused on a new initiative which will involve closer cooperation and deeper and more meaningful interaction between members of the two communities. The initiative, formally named 'Wings of

---

[1] This article was published by *Islam Today* in March, 2017, available online at: http://islam-today.co.uk/among-brothers-and-sisters-of-different-faiths.

Unity', will attempt to move away from the formalism and elitism often associated with formal interfaith activities. The first round of Wings of Unity discussions took place in July 2016 and the second was planned for January 2017.

During the Wings of Unity II conference, Prof. Coda delivered a talk entitled "An Epochal Change: The Culture of Unity in Chiara Lubich". After this talk, Dr Shomali presented on how love for God leads to love for one another. This was followed by a fruitful exchange of comments and ideas by participants who come from a variety of backgrounds. The message of unity was reinforced, and the programme concluded with a planning session for future collaborations, including an upcoming summer course in the city of Trent, where Catholics and Shias will have the unique opportunity to experience the "dialogue of life" and build on their understanding of unity of God and unity in God.

In addition to Wings of Unity II, Dr Shomali was invited to deliver a series of three lectures on Islam, Unity and Peace. The first series was delivered in April 2016. On the eve preceding his academic engagement, Dr Shomali (along with other guests who accompanied him) attended a Q&A session with members of the Focolare community, including students of the university. The theme was "Frontiers in Interreligious Dialogue". The guests were warmly welcomed by Prof. Bennie Callebaut who briefly explained the purpose of their visit before asking Dr Piero Coda, the President of the Institute, to say a few words. After welcoming the guests,

Dr Coda explained in a very personal and heartfelt tone that Dr Shomali's visit goes beyond the academic engagement.

Below is the text of what Prof. Coda said:

> I only want to say that we are very happy to have Dr Shomali here. This is the second time he has come to give lessons here and we consider him a member of the faculty; our visiting professor. He will give some lessons tomorrow on a course we have, where different religious representatives explain how they are working for peace and fraternity. This is a lovely experience and quite a unique course on the university stage. In addition to this, I have to say that we have another initiative, a kind of gift from God. Today before dinner we prayed together and we renewed our pact of unity that we made in July. In this beautiful place God has made us feel the friendship and brotherhood. Last year when Dr Shomali came to give his lectures, he came to my office, and I am not sure how it happened but we spoke for two hours and we came to the realization that we needed to deepen this dream that is a reality of the unity that comes from God and makes us walk together. Something clicked. I remember that Bennie was also there. We said that we

must do something together. I felt that this was something coming from God and that we have to do something about it. We looked at the calendar for a possible date for a meeting. I felt this was something God was asking us to do. July came up as an agreeable date. We asked ourselves: *What shall we name this new initiative?* This walking together to understand the source of Unity that is God, who is present in all of our religious experiences, where we share in the charism of Chiara. We all identify with it because it is not only Christian but belongs to all. To this question Mohammad without hesitation said, "Wings of Unity". So the Wings of Unity initiative was born in Sophia. We met for three days in July with a small group from the seminary – 12 people. We deepened our understanding of unity from our two points of view. This was an experience of profound unity from which we were motivated to go forward and transmit to the new generations this passion and this path for unity. This also gave birth to the idea of having a summer school where 20 Muslims and 20 Christians will study together. This will be held 90% at Tonadico where Chiara first had this inspiration for unity. Therefore, Shomali is here not only to give his lesson but to continue our walk, and in the following days we will explore other ways to deepen our experience. This is a beautiful thing that brings the Islamic Centre of England and Sophia University Institute closer together; God has placed a pearl in our hands.

Below is a summary of the Q&A session that followed. This session was entitled, "Frontiers in Interreligious Dialogue."

Q: *I am studying Trinitarian Ontology. Could you tell us why you got involved in interreligious dialogue and what dialogue means to you?* [Pietro from Bologna]

A: Our interest in dialogue came very naturally. We did not have any kind of training, any kind of mandate, or any experience. In 1997 we were in Manchester, UK, and we thought that since we're living in a prominent Christian country, we have a good opportunity to learn about Christianity. So in addition to our studies, we tried to find friends among Christians with whom we could have dialogue. At the time we were just looking for friends, but we ended up finding brothers and sisters. Interestingly, it was through the Focolare that we were introduced to Christianity, the Catholic Church, and other denominations.

Now almost twenty years after our initial involvement in interreligious dialogue, I can see that although we had no experience or prior knowledge, God helped us to come together. In the process, we found many people in our community who also appreciate having dialogue, and they have joined us in our journey. Thanks to God, we can now go forward.

We have reached a point that not only do we look at interreligious dialogue as a necessity in our lives in the twenty-first century, but we also see it as a deep responsibility towards God and humanity. We hope that through this important initiative, *Wings of Unity*, in Sophia, we will be able to prove to God our deep thirst for understanding what He asks of us in order to pave the way for the unity of humanity.

If we really struggle in the way of God, He will help us, and this means using all of the resources at our disposal, including holding discussions with you and trying to benefit from you, your resources, and your wisdom. And the same goes for you. I cannot only be active in my own circle and communicate with my Muslim sisters and brothers and then tell God that I have exhausted all my energy in understanding what He wants from us. But if we work together with openness and humbleness, then we no longer bother about whether the initiative comes from me or you - that won't be important at all. It is important that we open ourselves to God and He will help us to understand what the next step is. So I think this is a great gift of God, and if He finds value in us, He will help us to share this gift with other people who are very much in need of knowing about these initiatives.

The very fact that we are so close and we feel like one family is important; the intensity and strength we get from our unity is what the people of the world should know about, and I hope that with your support, energy and input the next generation will go even further.

Q: *Could you tell us about the differences between the Shi'a and the Sunni traditions?* [Trisha from Madagascar]

A: One of the moments in my life that I remember well is in 2004 when I went to Tehran airport to welcome four Catholic friends who were coming from the UK. One of them was the Jesuit Michael Barnes from Heythrop College. It was two in the morning when he asked me about the difference between Shi'a and Sunni Islam. I answered him in a way that he remembered, and referred to it later on many occasions. I told him: Of course, I am very much committed to Sunni and Shi'a unity, and I don't want to appear as someone who is proud of being Shi'a and underestimates the greatness of Sunnis. We are all brothers and sisters, and we have a lot in common, but something that I have noticed and I have shared with many people is that while we do have some theological differences related to the issue of the successor to the Prophet, the Shi'a have a kind of trinity. We believe in spirituality, rationality and the search for justice. Spirituality is very important for us, but spirituality joined with rationality. We have a great interest in philosophy, logic and intellectual reasoning; even in our seminaries we spend years studying philosophy, and we believe that reason and revelation supplement each other; they don't replace or contradict each other. We believe that God guides us both through the intellect and revelation. Also, we are very concerned about social justice. So if you can combine spirituality, rationality and seeking justice, you are in spirit a Shi'a even if you are a Sunni or a Catholic. And if you don't have these three, you are not a Shi'a even if you are called a Shi'a. I believe that these three elements are something that all religious traditions may find useful because if we only have spirituality without rationality, we might isolate ourselves from the realities of life. And sometimes our spirituality can be very superficial too. Rationality without spirituality becomes very dry; I cannot think of any religion that is without spirituality. And if we have spirituality without bothering about social justice, the issue of poverty, lack of opportunities for a great percentage of the people... this also would be a deficiency. So we should have all these together. If we have these three, we can also avoid extremism.

Q: *How can we confront extremism in religion and its consequences? What initiatives are taking place in the Muslim world? How can Christians and Muslims cooperate for changes in this area?* [**Andrea from Turin**]

A: It is a sad reality that in the course of history many sacred ideas have been misused. Religions, science and technology can all be misused, and Islam is no exception, especially now that Islam is widely spread, and there is vitality and an energy in the Muslim population. It is possible that some people or even a single person, do wrong and that can have an impact.

So despite the fact that Islam is a religion of peace, you find people who have such a misunderstanding that they think they have a call from God to use force and violence against people of no faith or other faiths – to the extent that even Muslims, their co-religionists, are victimised. It might be difficult for you to understand but I think you can imagine how this might happen since you also had a similar experience in Christianity. For these people, Muslims who are not with them are hated more than people of other religions. For example, for them killing a Shi'a is better than killing a Christian or a Jewish person. They are told that if they kill a Shi'a, they will go straight to Heaven. How can this idea exist? Is it because of Islam? No, because if religion was the cause we would have had a high percentage of Muslims who are like this. In reality, these people do not make up even a small fraction of Muslims. This behaviour is due to a mentality; they happen to be Muslim but could well have been Christians, Buddhists, Jews, or atheists. Today no religious tradition is immune. Extremism can come to any household. It can enter any religion; no matter how spiritual, peaceful or committed to love you are, extremism can come.

So there are many things that we have to do. First of all, as you mentioned, religious people have to work together and not allow anyone to use us against each other. That is the worst thing that can happen. It would be a waste of our energy and it can also give excuses to these people. They don't want us to be friendly; the worst things for terrorists are these kinds of meetings. Terrorists want to show that we are enemies, but we are insisting that we are sisters and brothers.

So we should work together on interfaith and interreligious programmes. Each community has to work hard to offer a proper education. When you hear about some youths who are involved in terrorist atrocities, you will notice that they were not religious people. They didn't go to the mosque or attend Islamic lessons. Some of these people have no religious background. That is why they are prone to being manipulated and brainwashed. They have a deep sense of guilt for not practising their faith. That guilt has been building over the years, and now all of the sudden they want to go to Heaven.

Education is very important. We need to invest in education as well as a good family environment. We need to safeguard families. One of the greatest challenges is the break-down of families. There is evidence to suggest that those involved in acts of atrocity are people who are not brought up in good families. They spend more time with their peers than their brothers, sisters and parents.

Another important factor is community. If Muslims, as a minority in the West, belong to a strong community that looks after its members and is concerned about individual development, then it can be very helpful.

This is a very serious issue. Certainly everyone, including Muslims, has the responsibility to think about it and we have to do our best to deal with people who are already affected and most importantly, to prevent the spread of these ideas which can spread in any tradition or ideology. What we need is *sophia* or wisdom. We don't need weapons or bombs; that will just add to the problem. Nothing can spread violence but extremism. Extremists feed on this, so we have to be very careful.

Q: *We know that you are conducting an academic activity of dialogue and research together with the Sophia Institute. Can you tell us how it is progressing? Also, what should we expect in the future from dialogue between Christians and Muslims?* [Donmarco Leone from Sicily].

A: This is a very good question that does not have a brief answer. Based on my theological and spiritual reflections and experiences, I believe that the future of the world very much depends on how Christians and Muslims work together. I am not saying something that I don't understand the implication of. It is a huge claim to make, but it is something that I've thought about very carefully.

Unfortunately, for the most part throughout history, Christians and Muslims did not work together as partners. There are many examples of peaceful existence but not fellowship. Perhaps on academic or business levels Islam continued on its own path and so did Christianity. In some cases they even competed with each other, like two suppliers who look at the same market and say this market is yours or the other is mine and we have to fight over it. This is a sad reality. The plan of God is not this. His plan is not to give us different books or religions to fight among ourselves, or merely to tolerate each other. In fact, God's plan is to have all of us together around the truth. But He does not force his plan.

As I humbly look at the world today and think of the future, I believe that there won't be any future for us if we continue in this way. There are so many challenges for us in the world today, and they affect all of us. If we want to work on our own and rely solely on our own resources, then we will not be able to cope with all of these trials.

I don't believe that in any part of the history of religions you can find faith and accountability before God being as ridiculed as it is in today's world. I don't think we have ever had so much immorality presented to us as 'normal' as well as a matter that we should not dare question, let alone criticise.

The only way forward for us is to get together and offer a joint testimony of faith in God to the people of the world. If Muslims and Christians work together and show how faith has brought unity, solidarity and brotherhood, then other people will be interested too. But if we boycott each other and attack each other's ideas, then there won't be any future for Islam or for Christianity.

Sometimes I count our blessings for these outside pressures and attacks on us because it has brought us closer together, and now we are realising the danger and realising that we cannot tackle it on our own.

For the last three years that I have been based in London, my real challenge has not been, for example, how to deal with a Shi'a becoming Sunni, a Christian or a Hindu. My challenge is our youth. Are our youth appreciative of our traditions? Are they able to be successful citizens of this society and at the same time have their own identities? Are they able to uphold family values? Are they able to maintain human relations in an age in which everything is digital and social networking and human relations are very much affected? These are the main challenges. The challenge is in helping those whose name or affiliation is Islam to have the true spirit of Islam. I think it is the same for Christianity.

Inter-religious dialogue is not something we do because it's fashionable or because we want to avoid war or fighting; rather, it is a necessity and it comes naturally to us. It is only one of many levels of work that we have to do. We have just started with this dialogue but we don't end it here. Thanks to God, we have gone very deep into this sense of unity with the Focolare in particular. It is much more than just dialogue.

I remember last time when we had the seventh round of Muslim-Christian dialogue; we said that perhaps instead of dialogue we should say 'dia-love'. We don't just talk to each other. We love each other.

I am sure this dialogue will happen, sooner or later, and we will see Muslims and Christians very close to each other. But I wonder in which generation we will be able to achieve it? God is patient; He gives us the opportunities. I believe that if we act properly and we have *sophia* [wisdom], it wouldn't take as long. The Qur'an says, "Indeed they see it to be very far, but we see it to be very near" (70:6-7). If we follow the path of God, then it is very near, but if we follow the path of humanity, then it is very far. So we ask God to give us from His own wisdom so that we may make this journey short.

[The session was closed with some reflections/prayer from Dr Piero Coda which reflects the atmosphere of the event.]

Piero: We should thank each other for having opened ourselves to God, and this is perhaps the most important thing for the world today. Whenever two or more people get together in the name of God, He will make His presence felt. When God shows Himself, all reality become present in that place. In Him we have been present here this evening as brothers and sisters in a world that cries, screams, is a prisoner of ideology, and suffers hunger, war, loneliness, violence, poverty... In doing what we can by creating spaces in which God is present, He makes us His witnesses. We have laid a stone in the construction of unity and peace for the entire world. The places in which this materialises, becomes, in that moment, the centre of the world where God is present. We thank our guest for having brought this reality; this gift that without you, your presence and effort only to build this unity not for money or human glory but for building together the presence of God which means simplicity, fraternity, liberty and purity. This is Unity. Therefore, we thank God who has willed this; He has 'put His tent among us' to use an expression from the Hebrew scripture. Now we do not wish to undo it wherever we are. This is the tent of wisdom. We thank you for giving us this presence of God that we have experimented and carry with us in our hearts and will keep for days to come.

Piotr Zygulski (student at Sophia University): *I would like to share these reflections with you. I see these days as an opportunity for conversion. But not as it was understood before, in an apologetic and limited way: we widen the horizon even of the word "conversion", as Professor Shomali widens that of the word "Islam" and how Christians in recent decades are dilating the conception of Christ. Well, we could convert all nations, beginning with us, yet we must not convert others to our identity - "a religion which is auto-identitarian is no longer the house of God," said Piero Coda - but we should let ourselves be converted and purified, together, by the one God, the source of our unity, who speaks also with the mouth of our brethren, whether they are "from Rome or Qom". This opens spaces for a co-conversion, a mutual and fraternal conversion. Perhaps only in this way you can understand today the invitation to conversion.*

Farha Iman (student at Sophia University): *The discussion between Dr. Mohammad Shomali and Don Piero Coda was very enriching and inspiring. After hearing them, I felt that their discussion was far more mature and inclusive than we're used to hearing. Their discussion made me comfortable and happy that there are people who talk, feel, and think in a similar way, and I think this is what the world needs the most. I believe the world is waiting for this kind of thinking and belief system.*